The Open Spiral of Life

a book
of poetry
by

HOLLY L.O. HUYCK

"The Open Spiral of Life—a Book of Poetry"
by Holly L.O. Huyck

Published by:

 RIO GATO
PRODUCTIONS
P.O. Box 2861-16 • Lakewood, CO 80228

PRINTED IN THE USA

First Edition

Book and Cover Design by David M. Pratt
Fort Collins, Colorado

ISBN 0-9662308-1-7

ABOUT THE AUTHOR

Holly Huyck is a geologist who lives with her husband and young son in Colorado. She has written poetry since the age of eight years and particularly since 1980. She has lived in many parts of the U.S. and spent more than two years of her adolescence in Costa Rica. She attended Carleton College in Minnesota, where she deepened her love of Shakespeare, honed her skill in drawing, and developed her enthusiasm for geology. She received her Ph.D. in geology from U.C. Berkeley in 1986, taught at a university for several years, then moved to Colorado and became a consulting geologist and a mother. She has worked both in mining and environmental geology. These poems reflect her experiences and observations in a varied life.

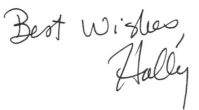

Best Wishes,
Holly

FOREWORD

The title of this book, and of one of its poems, is inspired by a passage from a book about grieving by the Reverend Dr. Alla Renée Bozarth. Her book, titled Life is Goodbye/Life is Hello: Grieving Well Through All Kinds of Loss, discusses the possible return of "aftershocks" five or twenty years after the initial loss. She notes that "a person may have to face this same old loss on new terms," but continues:

"The pattern is not that of a closed circle which you must repeat again and again, but an open spiral, moving ever outward and inward, returning ever anew to the same points of meaning, ever expanding outward from them." [1]

I consider this pattern to hold true for life itself, as well as for cycles of grief. Throughout life we each experience cycles of joy and sorrow, of birth and death, and of growth, plateau, and decline. We progress forward in age, even as we expand or contract our world. There are beginnings, middles, and endings in each cycle, as well as in our lives.

The poetry in this book is organized around three common stages: beginnings (birth/infancy), middles (adulthood), and endings (decline/death)... and new beginnings (resurrection). Each section focuses on stages of life. The middle section is subdivided into personalities and places.

This subdivision of life reflects my own evolution in other ways. As with all children, I first focused on bodily sensations, then emphasized my mind, and now, at midlife, am beginning to honor the soul and the balance among all three facets:

[1]p. 96, Life is Goodbye/Life is Hello: Grieving Well Through All Kinds of Loss, © 1982, revised edition 1986 by Alla Renée Bozarth, published by Hazelden Foundation.

BALANCING ACT

Once upon a time,
There lived
Three parts
Of one whole:
Body, mind, and soul.

In the beginning,
Body ruled.
Life was all new
Sensations, reactions,
Experiments, discoveries.

As body grew, mind began
To emerge.
Mind looked around,
        read the news,
        watched TV,
        observed the culture.

Mind was smart
And quickly realized
That males were more valued
Than females.
Mind decided to overcome body
By belittling female,
By being as logical
        and quantitative
        as possible.
This worked for a while,
Even though body
Was frequently ill.

With age, soul matured.
Soul channeled the repressed
Emotions and sensitivities
Into poetry, prose, and drawings.
Soul recognized that Mind
Had imprisoned Body.
Soul searched for a way
To unlock Body's prison
And found the key:
        Self-respect.
But Mind had monopolized
What little self-respect remained.
Mind feared the shifting balance
        and fought back
        with all the derogatory names
        that Mind could conjure
        for Body and Soul.

Soul, the mediator
In this long-standing feud,
Reminded Body and Mind
Of the need for balance
Among all three.

And here we sit,
Struggling for internal Peace,
And balance of Power
Among Body, Mind, and Soul.

Part of that balancing act is learning to accept my more soulful, sensitive, and wild side. I have always been likened to a cat; in fact, my childhood family nickname was "Kitten." Recognizing that part of myself, however, is different from embracing it and its inherent power:

EMERGENT PANTHER

My wild side
Was always present
As a tendency
Towards athleticism,
Towards natural settings,
Towards innovation,
And away from convention,
Or concrete walls,
Or old rules.

For years,
My wildness was caged
By my own fears
Of being different,
Until I realized
That my nature
Is to be different.

Now, my unfettered soul,
Strong and wild and soft
As a panther,
Is emerging from the shadows,
Albeit slowly, cautiously,
      creepingly.

One of my feline features is a strong need for privacy. Yet, my poetry necessarily entails a baring of my soul. Having spent my professional life in the earth sciences, where women are a distinct, and sometimes a token minority, I have learned to maintain strong defenses to protect my sensitivities from the daily onslaught of overt and covert disrespect — not from all corners, but enough to wear a soul down. So this book is difficult to share with the world. It could shock some who see me as a cool, logical, demanding doctor of science. It will not surprise my friends and confidants, however, who have encouraged me to take this daring step.

One administrative item is necessary to note. I do not consider "he" to include both sexes. I initially used "s/he" for a generic pronoun, but my reviewers considered that to be a distraction. Instead, I alternate "he" and "she" in the poems, and sometimes within a poem. I hope that the reader will not assign a specific gender to the subject in these poems.

— H.L.O. Huyck

ACKNOWLEDGEMENTS

To my friends, mentors, husband, and son, I owe the inspiration and strength to create this book. To the reader, I hope that the poems will provide humor, reflection, and power.

I particularly wish to thank the members of the "Rockettes," a monthly gathering of geologically oriented intelligentsia, who encouraged me to assemble my poems into a book and who occasionally tweaked the wording of individual poems. Three readers, Alla Bozarth, Nin Bebeau, and Leslie Landefeld, were responsible for helping to make this book a reality.

To Alla Renée Bozarth—godmother, poet, priest, and mentor—I owe the strength to follow my calling in both science and poetry. At the age of 27, Alla was the youngest of the eleven women to be ordained to the Episcopal priesthood in Philadelphia in 1974. Jeannette Piccard, the oldest of the "Philadelphia Eleven" at the age of 79, had a Ph.D. in chemistry. These two remarkable women are the subject of "Afternoon Lesson in Life—With Jeannette and Alla."

To Nin Bebeau I also owe the courage to follow my calling. Her creative counsel and ritual midwifery have been key to this book. Leslie Landefeld, a fellow mining geologist and Rockette, brought a scientific and down-to-earth perspective to reviewing this book.

I thank Alla, Nin, and Leslie for kindly reviewing the content and organization of these poems. Their encouragement and keen sense of flow in language greatly improved this book. Laine Gerritsen edited the book for grammatical consistency with sympathy for poetic expression. Carolyn McCant's proofreading polished the text to a fine luster. Despite their suggestions, however, I take full responsibility for the results, as I followed their sage advice selectively. David Pratt provided the visual design and artistic sensitivity for the book. I have often counted on his creativity for visually pleasing and stimulating designs.

August 28, 1997

THE OPEN SPIRAL OF LIFE

A book of poetry by H.L.O. Huyck, in three parts

FOREWORD AND ACKNOWLEDGEMENTS

BEGINNINGS

MIDDLES (PERSONALITIES)

MIDDLES (PLACES)

ENDINGS . . . AND NEW BEGINNINGS

BEGINNINGS

FREEFALL

Pregnancy is freefall.
We know the point where we jumped,
But we know not where we will land.
We only sense that
      a two-point takeoff
      will end in a three-point alighting.

At first, the freefall
      was nauseating and disorienting.
Eventually, my body adjusted,
      and turned to growing heavier,
      toward an increased sense of gravity,
Tugging self and soul ever more quickly
Toward that landing.

Are we ready?
Will we crash?
We fly on in unknowing.
We prepare,
Knowing we can never be prepared.

It's a time of hope and fear,
A time of joy and sorrow,
A time of great change and sought stability,
A time of wonder and banality,
A time of freefall.

AND THE WAIT GOES ON

...And the wait goes on
With daily grinds
    of weighted waddling
    of sleep deprivation
    of concerned anticipation.

I await your arrival, my child,
with mixed feelings.
I know that you are
    safe,
    active,
    nourished,
    growing,
    unaware of the outside.
As the wait goes on.

I know that I must
    climb a mountain,
    endure the physical equivalent
    of a grueling doctoral candidacy exam,
    pass through intense transition,
    and push you through to the other side.

I have often used the analogy
    of childbirth
For finishing a doctoral program;
Now, I use the latter
To gird my loins for your arrival.
And the wait goes on.

I gather hope that I can persevere
Through childbirth
Just as I completed
These other daunting tasks.

We have practiced and prepared,
We have nursery ready,
We have suitcases and stereo ready,
We have phone lists and diaper piles ready,
We know that we will never have everything ready,
Yet the wait goes on.
And we wonder when you will be ready
To show your tiny face to us
    and to join us
    in the outside world.

LABOR AND DELIVERY *

She labored
    deep into the night,
Eyes focused
    on nothing in particular,
Eyes sinking deeper
    with mounting exhaustion.
Waves of pain
Gathered in strength, length,
    and frequency,
Washing through her
Like a typhoon.
By morning,
The storm peaked
With a mother's cry of effort
    and welcome to a new life,
    and a newborn's cry of separation.

She labored
    deep into the night,
Eyes focused
    on nothing in particular,
Eyes sinking deeper
    with mounting exhaustion.
Waves of numbness
Gathered in strength, length,
    and frequency,
Washing through her
Like a warm fog.
By morning,
The fog enveloped her fully,
And she slipped away
    in silence
To another world and a new life.

* Dedicated to
my long-time
companion
and comforter,
Malachite, a
tortoise-shelled,
long-haired cat
who died the
day before my
son was born.

EYES OF THE STORM

I. GATHERING STORM

It begins with rising tides
That slowly wash over the body
For hours or days,
Portending the coming storm.
These signs are welcomed
With a mix of hope and anxious resolve.
Soon, the fury begins to build.
Waves of pain wash over one.
"Ride the waves. Give into them;
    Don't fight them."
The waves begin to crash rhythmically.
"This is your power. Welcome it;
    Don't shut it out."
A torrent of sweat accompanies the waves,
And screaming winds blow by.
"That's fine. Screaming is good;
    groaning is better."
As the storm intensifies,
    knives of pain slash at the body,
    tearing it apart.
Here, transition is a continuous
    searing of the soul,
As contractions shift from opening to pushing.
Sweat still pours down,
And waters break with a great gush.
But, we are close to the eye of the storm.
Pushing finally provides release,
And a child emerges.

II. THE EYE

After the fury of childbirth,
And in the midst of the storm,
    Is a child.
With blue-grey eyes
The color of coastal storm clouds.
All eyes and mouth,
He is the center
Around which all else whirls.
The few hours of relative calm
    after delivery
Include rest for the parents,
Brief instructions from staff,
And nourishment
Before the family is sent home
To face the other side of the storm.

III. THE OTHER SIDE

The gathering storm was internal—
    a wrenching apart of the mother's body.
This side is external—
    the fury of a newborn's needs.
This side is less intense,
    but lasts for weeks.
Each day is a new crisis
Confronted in a fog of little sleep.
Baby feeds every two hours;
Mother's milk does not come in or dries up,
      making nursing
        a screaming exercise
            in futility;
Baby becomes dehydrated
      or has digestive trouble;
Baby has jaundice or swallowed merconium;
Baby has blocked tear duct or eye infection;
Baby has incomplete digestive tract.
Baby provides howling winds,
Amid a torrent of tearless cries
      and full diapers.
Gradually—ever so slowly—the storm subsides,
As parents and child adjust
To a constant onslaught of needs
But an improving schedule
      and a more defined pattern.
Slowly, confidence in each other builds
And tides of anguish subside.
They will never stop;
Low tide will never be
    as calm as before.
Yet the stormy-eyed child
Will bring other high tides to life.

THE EYES HAVE IT

I.

Newborn,
I see the eyes
    of an old man
In your grey-blue eyes.

Old man,
I see the eyes
    of rebirth
As your body ebbs away.

Bodies come and go,
But spirits endure
And shine through the eyes
    of infants and aged alike.

II.

Newborn,
You drink in the world
Through blue-grey pools.

MOLTING

Two weeks post-term,
He entered this life
Looking like an old man.
Skin was wrinkled and cracked;
Limbs were thin and fragile.

Two weeks of age,
He is shedding his newborn skin
To expose the soft, supple shell
    that most people imagine
    in young infants.
Limbs are becoming plump and agile.

Many years of age,
He is shedding his adult skin,
As crow's feet and laugh lines
    become translucent.
Limbs are thin and fragile.
Skin lightens and body ebbs
To expose the spirit
And to ease its journey to the next life.

The molting cycle continues
As we shed the skins
    of each life
And our spirits move
    to the next world.

SECOND WIND

The midwife will tell you
At some point during labor,
When you feel fully spent,
That you must dig deeply
For your second wind;
That second effort
    is essential
To your child's birth.

HOWEVER,
This is only the first
Of second winds
That parenting requires.

When the baby wakes
In mid-night
For the hundredth time,
And you drag to her aid,
You need your second wind.

When the baby cries for hours
In obvious distress,
With no known cause,
You need your second wind.

When the baby cheerily stays awake
Both night and day,
Soaking up your aid,
    energy, and attention
With relentless charm,
You need your second wind.

When the baby rests,
You need a second wind
To wash, to prepare food,
    to change soiled bed
    or changing table,
    or to feed yourself.
She arises, refreshed,
While you search
For a third or fourth wind.

No wonder parents are so winded.

DROPPING IN

"Once you have a baby,
Nothing else will matter,
And you will want
To stay home full-time."

Predictions of my dropping out
Have been greatly exaggerated.
Yes, I want to spend time
With my child,
     to enjoy his daily discoveries,
     to recover from the trauma
        of childbirth.

But, as I recover,
My other talents
     begin to call.
Like muscles,
Once well-exercised,
That twitch with disuse,
My intellectual talents
Create irritating ticks
Until I exercise them.

Am I a bad mother
For needing to work
Outside the home?

NO.

I bring a greater richness
And a more relaxed approach
To my child
If I take the time
To "drop in" to work.

This balance of time
Is a costly challenge.
Yet, to let my other talents
     atrophy
Would insult my Creator
And further stress my child.

FATHERHOOD

Traditional fathers
Work hard to support
    families financially,
Spending long hours
    away from home,
And returning
For respite only.
They talk to children,
    or play hard
At their convenience.
They leave most parenting
    to the mothers,
Believing that raising children
Is easier
Than feeding them.

Nontraditional fathers
Work hard to support
    families in many ways,
Spending long hours
    outside the home,
But returning to help
    harried mothers.
They listen to children,
    or play hard,
    or change diapers
As needed,
Even when inconvenient.
They share much of the parenting
    with the mothers,
Realizing that raising children
Is as hard
As feeding them.

INFANT'S CHARM

Guileless smile
Of pure joy
Wipes away
        exhaustion
From tearier times.

Infant's laughs
Spring forth
With careless joy
And refresh
Aging adults.

BABY'S LAUGH

Pure joy
Without pretension
Or agenda.

Lust for life
In present tense.

Giggles rain down
Like a spring storm
Renewing life
In all beings.

Silliness,
But not at the expense of others;
Simple pleasure,
Without wit.

At what age
Does that laugh change?

INFANTS ARE NATURAL SCIENTISTS

What is this thing?

Is it big or little?
Is it heavy or light?
Can I pick it up?
(Will Mom or Dad say "NO!"?)

What does it look like?
What color is it?

What does it feel like?
Is it smooth or bumpy?
Is it sharp or round?

What happens when I push on it
    with my finger?
Does it slide or roll or bounce?
Is it hard or mushy?
Can I smear it on my face?
Can I smear it on a pet or a rug?

What happens if I step on it?
Does it change shape?
Does it spurt all over?

What happens if I bite it?
(Will Mom or Dad say "NO!"?)
Is it soft or chewy or hard?
What does it taste like?
Is it sweet or sour?
Does it get sticky
    when I drool on it?

What kind of noise does it make —
    If I blow on it?
    If I squeeze it?
    If I bang it on the floor?
    If I throw it?
    If I throw it at a person or a pet?

What is this thing?

CHILDREN ARE STRANGE ATTRACTORS *

I.

"Children are strange attractors."

They bring chaos
To the once-ordered
Lives of adults,

Or compound chaos
For adolescents.

As soon as a pattern
Is observed or surmised
   —in infant's sleeping habits,
   —in toddler's eating habits,
   —in youngster's playing habits,
   —in teen's social habits,
IT CHANGES!

* *In mathematics,
"strange attractors"
are phenomena
characterized by
both order and
chaos.*

II.

"Children are strange attractors."

They are simultaneously
   —frustrating and beguiling,
   —exhausting and exhilarating,
   —deplorable and adorable.

They create an ever-changing
Rollercoaster ride
Of lows and highs,
Of twists and turns
    and screaming delights,
Of patterned chaos.
They mold their parents
As much as their parents shape them.

If children are strange attractors,
What does that make their parents?

In-Home Day Care

Each child's arrival
Is a ritual of
Laying-on-of-hands
By other children,
As they gather to
Hug, kiss, pat, and smile
Their greetings.

Although physical illness
Is commonly passed
In this ritual,
The spiritual soothing
Outweighs
Such inconveniences.

ALPHABET SOUP OF CHILDHOOD DISEASES

A is for appetite loss and antibiotics.
B is for bronchitis.
C is for colds, croupy coughs, and constipation.
D is for diarrhea and dehydration.
E is for ear infections.
F is for fevers and flu.
G is for gassiness and grumpiness.
H is for high fevers and hives.
I is for irritability.
J is for jaundice.
K is for Kleenex (strewn everywhere).
L is for laryngitis and listlessness.
M is for mumps and measles.
N is for nausea.
O if for otitis media (ear infection, again).
P is for pox, as in chicken.
Q is for queasy feeling.
R is for rubella and RSV (respiratory syncytial virus).
S is for snot, especially gooey and green.
T is for testiness and disease transmission
        (mainly to friends and parents).
U is for unclear diagnosis.
V is for vomiting and viruses galore.
W is for wheezing.
X is for excretions of all kinds.
Y is for yellow mucous.
Z is for z-less, as in lost sleep for parents.

Catching and carrying
This alphabet soup
Of childhood diseases,
Young children are
Walking Petri dishes.

TO MY TODDLER

Lean-limbed and Buddha-bellied,
She toddles towards me,
Grinning, arms outstretched.

LITTLE BEAR

Grazing among berries—
    blueberries,
    raspberries,
    strawberries—
He grunts happily
And smacks his lips.

Tumbling with friends,
He growls softly and swats playfully,
Eyes aglow
With the moment's joyful frenzy.

Ambling through fields,
He inspects flowers, trees,
    pebbles, weeds,
    insects, and seeds
With keen interest,
Observing, pawing, sniffing, tasting
This brave new world
With boundless energy.

Who is this Little Bear?
My young son.

IMAGINARY FRIENDS

I.

The infant looks back
To see if her mirrored image
Is still watching.

II.

The toddler brightens, smiles,
Waves, and says, "Hi!"
To her reflected image.

III.

Is a toddler's own
Mirror image
Her first imaginary friend?

LOSS OF INNOCENCE

When born to a loving family,
An infant develops
The assumption
That all people
Are good, and
All people
Like her.

Unwittingly, the infant
Follows unknown children
To greet them openly,
Often to be rebuffed
By cold stares
And puzzled looks.

As the infant progresses
Into knowledge-through-language,
She loses that
Loving innocence;
She learns that words
Can hurt, as well as heal,
And that many
Do not love her
For no good reason —
For her color, race, sex, shape, whatever —
For no good reason.

EMERGENCY...

He was awakened
In middle night
By a sharp cry of pain
And shuffling, bumping noises.
By the time his eyes
Were fully opened,
The next-door neighbor
Stood by his crib,
Stroking his hair and
Speaking soothing words.

He did not see his father
For twelve hours
Or his mother
For four days
(And then, only
In a hospital).

His secure world
Of routine safety
Was shattered
By the sudden sensation
That his ever-faithful parents
Could be taken from him
By an emergency.

For Brian

AND RESPONSE*

Within two weeks,
The toddler was transformed
From a typical two-year-old
To an independent assistant
For his ailing mother.

Shocked by the reality
Of life's fragility,
The toddler developed
An unusual independence.

When his mother came home
From the hospital,
He insisted on
        dressing himself,
        feeding the dog,
        running the microwave,
        and carrying food to the table.

How wonderful to see this shift
From self-centered child
Toward self-sufficient adult,
Yet how sad to watch it happen
So early and so quickly
To a bright, young child.

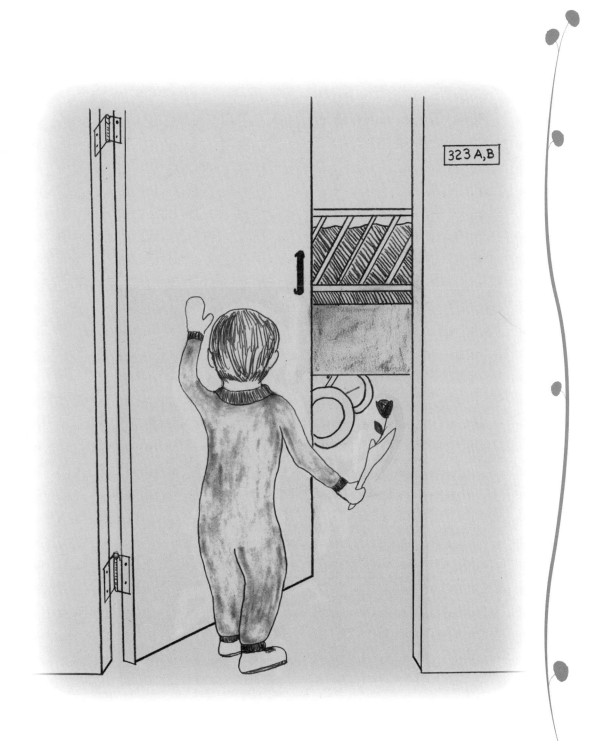

323 A,B

TERRIBLE TWOS

The terrible twos
Are merely rehearsal
For the turbulent teens.

NOVICE/EXPERT

During intoduction to
　　life, language,
　　society, culture,
　　arts, or sciences,
We learn the general rules.

We spend
The rest of our lives —
Social and professional —
Learning the exceptions.

The devil is in these details.

MIDDLES
(PERSONALITIES)

THREE R'S

The three R's—
Reading, wRiting, and aRithmetic—
Provide students with
The means of survival,
But the sciences
Provide joy-in-discovery,
And the arts
Provide the reasons for living.

Arts and sciences are as crucial
To liveliness
As the three R's are to livelihood.

THE MUSE *

The Muse is as erratic and powerful
    as a Wyoming thunderstorm.
She rarely comes
    when you feel parched
    and in need of rain.
Instead, when least expected,
She blows in,
    strikes you with lightning inspiration,
    then pounds you with hail
    until you respond.

Many are the sleepless nights
When she awakens me
With the hot strike of inspired concept,
Then drenches me
    until I rise
    and write the rushing thoughts down.
I often fight her stormy energy,
Tossing to calm a jumpy heart
    and a nervous mind.
Eventually, I give in to her.
Once the torrent of words
    is splashed onto paper with ink,
The storm subsides.
Flash floods of ideas
    quickly drain away,
And my inner landscape
    returns to mud-cracked drought
Until the next stormy visit
Of the Muse.

* Dedicated to Gretel Ehrlich, who knows
the inner "Solace of Open Spaces," and
to Alla Bozarth, who knows well the
late-night visits of the Muse.

BRAIDED STREAM *

I am a braided stream.
My source is the glaciers and snows of
    high mountains and alpine meadows.
My end is the Pacific Ocean.
Like the Platte River, I am changing—
Roaring, rushing river, overflowing banks
    and uprooting all in my path,
Or quiet eddies under aspen and willow trees.
I feel the strength of mountain and ocean
    in my extremities.
I feel the waters of life coursing through my veins.
I know the ancient wisdom
    of pre-existing mountains at my source's core.
I know the power of pounding surf in my legs.
I am life-giving to plants and creatures in my path.
I guide eroded sediments or souls
    to form new rocks of strength,
    and possibly new mountains, at my feet.
I can be destructive, if the banks holding me in
    are too restrictive.
Mostly, I braid intricate patterns of spirit-body-
    thought-action-creativity-achievement,
    for the attentive ones
    to see and enjoy and find nourishment.
My braids are long strands of algae, sand, and water.
I am deceptively quiet;
    those who do not take me seriously
    are likely to drown in my challenging currents.
Those who treat me with respect, who know my
    wisdom and power,
    will quench whatever thirst
    and find refreshment
    in my watery bed.
I am a braided stream, and I will NOT be dammed!

* *Dedicated to Loren Eisley, who respected "The Flow of the River" in* The Immense Journey.

30

BLOOD RIVER

I am the river of life.
I build gradually,
Then, periodically,
    I overflow,
Rushing, gushing, oozing,
I flush out all wastes in my path.

Occasionally,
    I remain.
Nurturing, feeding,
    breathing life into
    a new being-to-be.

Many traditions
    associate me with death,
    with otherness,
    with uncleanliness.
They have forgotten
    that without me
    there would be no life.

My children,
    REMEMBER
    where you came from!

I am the Cleansing,
    Creating,
    Sustaining
    River of Life!

BRIDGE

I am a bridge.
I carry an odd balance of yin and yang,
Both feminine and masculine,
Both scientist and artist,
Both old soul and new spirit.

As daughter and mother,
I span generations.
As geologist and poet,
I feel the science and dissect the text.
As traditionalist and feminist,
I honor old truths and celebrate new ones.

As a bridge,
I am anchored in opposing sides,
Yet arch freely over the roiling turmoil
    of their clashing schisms
    as they attempt to erode
    each other's foundations.
From my span, adversaries find new perspectives
And—just maybe—find hopeful middle ground
Of common purpose.

Yet, as a bridge,
I will not be abridged
Into one psychology or ideology,
And that drives opposing sides crazy!

WATER LULLABIES

Only recently have I discovered
My love of water lullabies.

Give me the sounds
    of waves thundering on a beach,
    of mountain streams burbling
       and gurgling downhill,
    of rain falling on rooftops in the desert,
    of loons crying on a quiet lake,
And I feel peace.

I have heard that
These sounds are soothing
Because they are "white noise."
    So is an air conditioner;
    So is static on the radio;
    So is the distant sound
       of highway traffic.
Yet these are not soothing.

Perhaps my body responds to water sounds
Because I am made mostly of water.

WATER LILY

Out of the murk, I RISE,
From muddy roots and dim pasts,
I strain towards light.
Achingly slowly, I grow upwards.
Reaching, twining my stem,
I carry ancient wisdom in my being.
I curl my stem for flexibility
     in changing water levels.
Unlike fast-growing reeds,
I develop slowly,
     weighted by wisdom,
     unhurried by passing floods or fads.
I will blossom some day.
For now, I must hold the vision
     of soft, white petals
     floating on green pads
As I stretch towards clearer water,
     towards light.
I am becoming what I was meant to be,
     being my calling,
     evolving,
     learning
That this is a process.
Life is not a goal, but a process.
I must celebrate each stage,
     even when the water is dark,
     and my spirit-light is hard to discern.

Water lily I   HLOH 7/18/15

REDWOODS

I.

Ancient redwoods are
Elegant examples
Of plodding persistence.

II.

A cluster of slender sisters
Circles the roots
Of their mother's grave.

III.

I am a redwood tree.
Tall and straight,
I tower above all
Except my kin.
Still young at 800 years,
I carry the scars
Of centuries-old
    fires and burrows.
My furrowed bark
Is thick, hard, and resilient,
To protect
My softer and nourishing
heartwood.
As I grew,
Other trees shot up
And blocked my view.
But fire and bugs
Laid them low
Eons ago.
I have slowly,
    inchingly,
Persevered.
Now my battle scars
Simply decorate
My lower trunk.
Change is inevitable,
But perseverance outlasts
Many transitions.

ROOTED FLIGHT

One of life's paradoxes
Is that
Those of us
    who are most grounded
    and best rooted
Soar,
While those of us
    who are uprooted
    in body or spirit
Plummet.

We seek our roots.
If we cannot find them,
We must learn to grow them,
    to let them sink deep into soil,
    to spread and intertwine with
        community,
    to gather nourishment for ourselves,
    and to provide nourishment for others.

A scientific study
Discovered that,
    in arid lands,
Some trees
Provide not only shade
But also water
To their thirsty neighbors.

Postscript:
**Blessed are the flighty,
For their rootlessness
Has clipped their wings.**

May our developing rootedness
    provide sustenance
    to ourselves and our neighbors,
And may the strength of our roots
Help us to SOAR
Above pettiness, injustice, fear, and oppression.

PIONEERS, PREGNANCIES, AND PH.D'S
(HARD LABOR, ALL THREE)

What do pioneers, pregnancies, and Ph.D's
Have in common?
The same threads bind these three:
Persistence, passages, and hard labor.

I. PIONEER

The journey of Pioneers
Across America
Was from eastern to western shores,
With many obstacles in between.

First, uprooting themselves
        from the swampy Atlantic shores,
Climbing the Eastern Piedmont,
Then finding passage
        through the Appalachian Mountains,
Then slogging through muddy forests and
        forging streams or rivers
        in the Midwest,
Then deepening rutted roads
        in treeless, windswept plains,
Then crossing over the Rocky Mountains,
Next passing, parch-lipped, through
        hostile, hot deserts
Only to find the Sierra Nevada or Cascade
        Mountains blocking their journey.

All this time,
The pioneer may have encountered
Hostile natives
Who were angered
By such intrusions
Into their territories.

If these obstacles were overcome,
The Central valley of California
    and the Coastal Ranges remained
Before sighting the glistening Pacific Ocean.

II. PREGNANCY

The journey of pregnancy
Begins in a sea
    of passion and conception.
Next, the gathering sense
    of knowing and unknowing,
    as the mother recognizes her state
    and seeks safe passage
    through morning sickness.
Then, if morning sickness ends,
The mother slogs through a long period
    of steady growth and distention,
    of mixtures of joy, fear,
        anticipation, and concern
    sweeping across her soul,
    as hormonal shifts sometimes
    leave her feeling uprooted.
As time continues, hot spells and thirst
    commonly characterize
    middle to late pregnancy.

After nine months of persistence,
Labor and delivery require
    the stamina and focus
    of surmounting the Sierra Nevada
Before she can see her new child,
    she glistening with sweat from work,
    and her child glistening with blood.

All this time,
The mother may encounter
Overzealous advice-givers —
Parents who believe
That only they
Know the right way
To mother.

III. Ph.D's

The journey of a Ph.D. student
Contains similar perils and lulls.
Upon entering school,
The student treads forward in coursework,
Searching for a thesis topic
    and an appropriate advisor
To guide her through the end.
She must find safe passage
    through the mountainous terrain
    of candidacy exams,
    where attaining new plateaus
    of understanding
    is requisite.

Then she must slog through many months
    of data collection,
    course correction,
    changing theories and emphases,
    plodding plots of graphs galore,
    ever-shifting outlines,
    and innumerable drafts.
This muddy process can,
In some cases,
Throw the student into ruts
    that permanently bog her down,
Or she may persevere,
Searching for pathways of insight,
Sometimes buffeted by changing winds
    of departmental politics
    (much hot air, dry of import).
At some midpoint,
A mountainous weight of doubt
    will test her resolve,
    and she must find
    another crossing point.
But this is not the end.
On the other side lies
    a desert of dissertation,
    a sense of no-end-in-sight,
    a thirst for clarity
    amidst many mirages.
Eventually, a shift occurs,
As the student finds yet newer levels
Of understanding and synthesis.
But completion of the thesis
    requires the stamina and focus
    of climbing the Sierra Nevada
    without being eaten alive
    by doubts or distractions.

The exhilaration of a completed draft
Is followed by the valley of rewrites
And, eventually, the last crossing
        of coastal mountains —
        the dissertation defense —
Before she can wash away her exhaustion
In the glistening waters
Of the sea at sunset.

All this time,
The student may encounter
Hostile members
Of the doctoral club
Who attempt to
Obstruct her passage
Into their hallowed territory.

JOBLESS

I.

The blurred vision
  and cold clamminess
  of self-doubt
Creeps upon me like a dense fog.
It chills me to the core.
It surrounds me,
  choking off
    my imagination,
    my initiative,
    my strength.
It saps all energy
Into infinite dissipation.
It numbs me
And disconnects me
  from my talents
  from self-knowledge
  from trust
    in anyone
    or anything,
    especially myself.
I huddle in this fog,
Hoping to survive
Until the confident sun
Burns it away,
And I can function again.

II.

I am so tired
of pounding my head
against brick walls.
NO job; not for me;
no, No, NO!
I'm so tired of "NO"!
I want to scream back
  "NO MORE!"

Long-term joblessness
Is slow water torture,
Each "no" another
Acid drip to wear me down.
Drip, drip.
No.
Drip.
No.
Drip.
Enough!
No more drips!
No more "No's"!

I thirst
  for the cleansing, clean
  water of a "Yes!
    You are just what we need!"
An affirmation
That my talents
Are useful in the world,
Useful enough to earn pay.

SQUEEZE PLAY

I.

A friend once said,
"You scare the miners
Because they
Cannot dismiss you
As a non-woman
Or as incompetent."
"You scare the miners
Because you
Do your job well,
Yet you have
A feminine essence
That they cannot ignore."

II.

You're too girlish!
 You're not soft enough!
You wear long hair!
 You don't wear makeup!
You're not aggressive enough!
 You're not demure enough!
You're not explosively strong enough!
 You're not supple enough!
You're too emotional!
 You're too cerebral!
You're not man enough!
 You're not woman enough!

III.

Caught between stereotypes
Of "successful" men or ladies,
With both sides trying
 to tag me as "out"
 of the game
For daring to be myself,
I struggle to finesse
This winless race.
I do not see a solution...
Unless I rewrite the rules.

WOMAN'S MANTRA
(A FEMININE NEUROSIS)

If something is wrong
In the world,
It must be my doing,
And I must fix it.

BUT
If something is right
In the world,
It must be someone else's doing;
I don't have that kind of power.

LIBERATION MEDITATION

To liberate myself
From negative self-image
And self-flagellation
That I absorbed
Since childhood,
I am replacing some old images
With new ones.

OLD IMAGES

A yoke signifies the notion
That happiness is punished;
I should never be too happy,
Or I will pay with greater pain.

A heavy coat of armor signifies
The requirement to be
Moderate in emotions
At all times,
Even when excess is appropriate.

A series of red and black hoops
Represents the constant trials
I face to prove myself
Over and over and over again
Through fire or painful tasks.

NEW IMAGES

A wreath of silver stars
In my hair signifies
Freedom to be full of JOY
Without anticipating retribution.

A full-length, layered, gossamer
purplish dress signifies
Freedom to express feelings fully
Whenever I need to,
Without fear of stifling castigation.

A rope-and-wood swing on an
expansive old oak tree
Represents freedom in self-knowledge
That I am competent, even excellent,
And can launch myself to great actions.

OLD IMAGES

A ladder with a clock at the top
Signifies society's stopwatch
For attaining success—
    financial or professional—
In a brief time.

Chocolate bonbons represent
My mother's image of
The epitome of the lazy,
    selfish mother,
Lounging on her sofa
While children are unheeded,
Unfed, or undisciplined.

Tight, dry, prickly skin
Represents moodiness and
    crankiness
Of an overwhelmed
Wife and mother,
Too drained for fun.

A vise represents pressure
To produce constantly,
Lest I be labeled selfish
    or lazy,
And the self-blame for
A pioneer whose chores
Are never finished.

NEW IMAGES

A silver and dark blue, braided barrette,
With matching tapestry shawl,
Signifies the many parts of my life
That intertwine into a complex pattern
Of triumphs over a lifetime.

Chocolate chip oatmeal cookies
Represent my image of
The caring, thoughtful mother
Providing her family with
Fun nourishment and
Attention to their needs,
As well as to hers.

Rubbery, soft, supple skin
Represents silliness and
    centeredness
Of a wife and mother
Who balances chores with frivolity
And others' needs with her own.

A torch represents inspiration
For a pioneer mother
Who is lighting the way
To a balanced life
    in which
Laughter and growth are as important
As a clean kitchen floor.

WARRIOR WOMAN

The warrior woman
Had survived
Decades of battles
     to succeed in a hostile society,
     to gain almost-equal footing
        with her male colleagues,
     to gain recognition
        for her many talents.

Her armor was
     dented,
     rusted,
     rigid
from effort.

Now the challenge was shifting.
Slowly, she removed her bruised body
     from the heavy load
     of metal and mail armor.
It had served its purpose
And had cocooned her (albeit harshly)
     for years.
The stiff protection, however,
Was becoming a prison;
It was time to emerge
     a different woman.
Her expanding body
     could no longer be held
     within such confines.

Like a newborn butterfly,
She inched gingerly
Out of the armor.
The transition was
     more complete
Than she had realized.

From a chrysalis of metal
Emerged a woman
Enveloped in golden light.
No wings here,
Rather a beautiful aura
    of gold-pink-peach
    and peaceful strength.

This new auramor
Would protect her
    even better,
Deflecting society's blows
Without dents or rust.

This new auramor
    was so light
That she could move FREELY,
Unencumbered by society's strictures.

She emerged, a warrior mother,
Stronger and fiercer,
But at peace and unrestrained
By the old rules.

Standing outside the rules
That she had followed
    for decades,
She laughed,
Bounced her new child on her breast,
And strode away from the old armor
To new adventure, freedom,
    and JOY.

WARRIOR WOMEN *

We warrior women
Are legion in number.
We carry power
    in many forms.

We withstand
    the vagaries of a
    patriarchal society.

We deflect the blows
    of inequality
    of injustice
    of prejudice
    of in-opportunity
To rise again.

And still we give birth
    to children,
    to poetry,
    to gardens,
    to scientific discovery,
    to new insights
        of a better world.

Each birth requires strength
    of mind,
    of body,
    of soul.

Each creation involves
    growing beyond old confines,
    loving and nurturing
    and laboring to give life
    to new ideas and beings.

We must recognize
Each other's strength
    in her creations,
For each endeavor requires
    endurance,
    invention,
    power,
    and breathing life
    into new form.

* Dedicated to ALL women who
strive, whether inside or
outside the home, whether in
traditional or nontraditional
ways, for a better world.

WARRIOR MEN *

Warrior men work beside
Us warrior women,
In the trenches,
   Washing dishes,
   Cooking dinner,
   Changing diapers,
   Changing oil,
   Raking leaves,
Before or after a long day's work.

They pursue a wayward toddler
With the same zeal
As capturing a new contract,
Handling a resistant snowplow,
Or subduing an unruly computer bug.

They support us
In our struggle
For equal opportunities
And in our breaking
Through old boundaries.

Warrior women
Will only win such battles
With help from our brethren,
   Mentors, friends, and lovers,
The warrior men.

(The other guys are just wimps.)

** Dedicated to my
warrior husband,
Daniel R.H. O'Connell.*

THREE LOVERS

The first lover
Had piercing blue eyes,
Full of vigor
And lust,
But little spirit.

The second lover
Had soft brown eyes,
Full of friendship
And spirit,
But little lust.

The third lover
Had intense green eyes,
Full of vigor,
      friendship,
      spirit,
And lust.

Those green eyes
Still flash
With enough love
To last a lifetime.

INSIDE OUT

So many of us
Spend our lives
As outsiders,
Looking in.

Some long to belong
To the inner circle,
Even as they know
They will never be invited
To share in its secrets of power.

Such longing, unfulfilled,
Can tear a person
From the inside out.

Others long to belong
To their own inner circle,
To celebrate the vibrancy
Of diverse origins
And common interests,
To become the inviters,
To compound their own power.

Such longing, fulfilled,
Can give voice
To the once-silenced.

Yet the new insiders
Must guard against
Creating new outsiders
And losing empathy
As they gain power.

Still others,
Slowly becoming accustomed
To outsidedness,
Learn to take pride
In their unique perspectives,
Viewing insider circles
With detached discernment.

This last group contains
The prophets of our times.

THOSE WHO ARE CALLED

To raise children well
And to give hope to the next generation
Is a noble and challenging calling
Which should be undertaken
Only by someone of great talent,
Stamina, patience, and insight.

To discover scientific breakthroughs
Which improve life's journey
Is a noble and challenging calling
Which should be undertaken
Only by someone of great talent,
Stamina, patience, and insight.

To forge a lasting peace
Which affirms all peoples' dignity
Is a noble and challenging calling
Which should be undertaken
Only by someone of great talent,
Stamina, patience, and insight.

To create artistic works
That give life meaning
Is a noble and challenging calling
Which should be undertaken
Only by someone of great talent,
Stamina, patience, and insight.

To guide lost souls to wholeness
And to celebrate each freed spirit
Is a noble and challenging calling
Which should be undertaken
Only by someone of great talent,
Stamina, patience, and insight.

When such callings
Require so much
Effort, persistence, and giftedness,
Why in the world
Would anyone limit opportunities
For those who are called
Merely on the basis
Of race, creed, or gender?

RAISING CHILDREN

Raising Children means:

Filling their expansive minds;
Feeding their busy bodies;
Encouraging healthy experiments
    while preventing excesses
    or healing accidental hurts;
Rejoicing in new accomplishments
And comforting wounded hands or souls;
Chasing wayward toddlers
Or prodding sluggish teens;
Diffusing fights
While shaping characters;
Rocking restless creatures to sleep
Or raising flagging spirits.

What duties could be more critical,
More joyful,
Or more taxing,
Than raising children?

To The Women's Mining Coalition

Well-grounded women,
They are daughters,
Mothers, grandmothers
Who dig Earth's bounty.

Solid,
Although they come in
All shapes and sizes,
Their rootedness
Stems from hard work.

Smiling,
They face hardship
And disdain
With resourceful aplomb.

Savvy,
They have learned
To work around
Or blast through
Physical and
        cultural barriers.

Who are these legions?
Why miners, of course!

To the Philadelphia Eleven — Twenty Years Later

Eleven sisters
Went out on a limb
To celebrate Wholeness.

Three brothers
Supported the limb
To consecrate a Whole Priesthood.

Two thousand people
Surrounded the tree
To witness healing
    of its brokenness.

Out of fear and despair
    came Joy;
Out of a church's wounds
    we were healed.

Many present that day
Paid dearly
    for daring
    to follow
    God's Call
In measured defiance
Of canonical rules.

Many who rejoiced that day
Are tired and bitter
After twenty years of struggle
To redefine and heal
    a once-broken priesthood.

Yet from that first limb,
Many more have branched,
And women and men
Who are called
To a Whole Priesthood
Continue to celebrate
    God's Word.

From eleven
First Female Disciples
Have sprung fifteen hundred.
The struggle for equality
    continues,
But the first branch
Remains strong
And blooms especially
    each Easter
    and Feast of Mary and Martha,
Despite many intervening
    winters of pain.

GRACE *

What is Grace?
The curve of a body,
The supple movement,
Taking Joy in living
    even when life
    is difficult,
God's relation with us,
Learning and living
    our individual calling.

Arthur Ashe,
A graceful Master
Of the tennis court,
Who broke color barriers
    with panache,
Broke other barriers
With Grace,
Even as his life ended.

Arthur Ashe,
Being strong enough to forgive
When forgiveness will help us all,
Grew in Grace,
Even in his last
Days of Grace,
Before AIDS took his life.

* *Inspired by "Days of Grace" by Arthur Ashe.*

58

DIFFERENCE OF OPINION

My black friends
Disagree with each other.

Some say that they
Face job discrimination
Because they are black.

Others say that they
Face job discrimination
Because they are women.

Why this difference of opinion?

The first group works
In traditionally female jobs.
The second group works
In traditionally male jobs.

Both groups work hard,
Despite the barriers they face
Every single day.

TO WOMEN'S INSTITUTE ON RELIGION AND SOCIETY *

A small
Rainbow of women
Began to meet monthly
To encounter the racism
Within themselves and within
Their larger life and community.

They discovered
How they perceived
Themselves and each other
In a motley variety of stereotypes.

They shared
Common and separate
Experiences with each other.

They owned
Their individual,
Long-imbedded racism
In order to dismantle the
Prejudice within themselves.

Some felt
That racism
Was only present
In the ruling (white) race,
Since it required having power.

Others felt
That racism
Was always present
In all races (white, brown, black, etc.)
Through universally internalized misperceptions
Of their own and other races.

Some fought
Over divisions of
Class and education.
(The white welfare mother
Accused the black professor
Of elitist rhetoric, for example.)
Often, these differences colored
Perceptions more strongly than race.
So, the women also worked on overcoming
These contrasts in the group's spectrum.

By working
To share those
Inbred animosities,
They slowly began to
Find common roots and insights
In being women of this world.

By struggling
With long-held anger
Towards previously unknown
Members of a class or a race,
They learned to forgive themselves
And each other for past societal wrongs,
And to commit to undoing ongoing oppressions.

By valuing diversities
And celebrating similarities,
They focused their rainbow of experience
Through a prism of understanding
To find a new and holy Light of
Hope, support, and action.

That new Light shines
In some small corners of
The world, where friends and
Allies are taking small steps
Towards respect for each other and
Towards healing ancient racial wounds.

*The Women's
Institute on
Religion and
Society was formed
in Cincinnati in the
mid-1980s.
It continued to
educate its
members and the
larger community
until it formally
disbanded in 1996.
Its bonds continue
informally.*

AFTERNOON LESSON IN LIFE—WITH JEANNETTE AND ALLA

In a sun-washed room
Of a Victorian home,
Three women sat and
    talked over tea.

Three life stages merged
On that frigid Minnesota winter's
    afternoon.

The oldest, snowy-haired,
With a wit as sharp as a scalpel,
Spoke of her upcoming birthdate
    with death
And her hope for entering in
    to a new life of joy,
    reunion,
    and freedom from sin.

She spoke of moving on
As though it were as easy
    as cleaning this room
    and entering the next.
A chemist and priest in her 80's,
She was ready
    to explore the next life.

The second woman
Was just reaching the blossom
    of her thirties,
Despite having the physical delicacy
    of a porcelain doll.

Her piercing intellect
Brought scripture and humor
    to this informal lesson.

A poet and priest,
She explored the nuances of
Body's spirit and soul's Word
That the others had not envisioned.

The third woman,
Just budding into her 20's,
    basked in the sunshine
        of that toasty room
    and in the day's Dance
    of mind and soul and more.

She wondered if she, too,
Was called to be a priest.
She glimpsed the Joy
That might have been Jesus'
When he first sat
    at the rabbis' feet
    in the Temple.
Holiness was palpably present.

Years later,
The oldest has died well,
The middle heals souls,
And the youngest
Has become a scientist and artist,
Exploring mountains and spirits,
Completing the interwoven,
    triumvirate circle
    of calling
That only now
Is becoming clear to her.

TIME OUT

It's time to take
A time out
From seriousness,
A time out
For silliness.

To frolic
To clown around,
To drop the all-too-steady
Seriousness of surviving
Like yesterday's laundry.

Let the everyday sobriety
Molder awhile in the hamper
As we unbutton our suits
And don layers of laughter
Tumbling over itself
And rustling in
Gales of giggles.

The ponderous world
Of adult concerns
Can wait a few minutes
While we refresh our souls
And remember why we bother
With the daily details
Of sustaining life.

It's time to take
A time out
For silliness!

CHOCOLATE

WHAT?!
Chocolate has
No nutritional value?!
It may not feed the body,
But it sustains the soul!

MIDDLES
(PLACES)

TRANSITIONS

I.

Moving forward, off-balance
In thick fog,
Unsure of destination.

II.

There is no going back,
Yet, ahead
Lies uncertainty
Of the unknown.

III.

Five new paths of choice,
Each with distinct endings,
Diverge from this old path.

IV.

With privilege of choice
Comes responsibility
Of decision.

V.

Where to go
In this sea of sand?
Even my tracks
Disappear in the dunes.

JULY 20, 1969

They gathered
From miles around
At the American Embassy;
Hundreds watched
A small TV screen
With pictures from the Moon.

Many were in
Guatemala City
For market day,
Having walked their goods in
On ox-drawn carts.
Half lived without
Electricity or plumbing.
They wore the bright patterns
Of Mayan descent.

Others came
In diplomatic limousines,
Fully bedecked
In designer fashions
And Rolex watches.

Yet, for one BRIEF moment,
All the assembled
Stood, transfixed
By the simple act
Of a man
Stepping on the Moon.

All were united
As Earthbound humanity,
Cheering at the sight,
Beaming at the screen,
Astonished.

An hour later,
The crowd had melted
Into its distinct classes
And separate worlds.

Spring Snow in the Black Forest

I.

Straying from the beaten path,
We crunched through
    last year's leaves
And ambled among
    skeletons of trees
Etched in an early spring fog.

II.

The fog thickened
To cream soup.
Black tree trunks
Eventually faded
    and disappeared
Only five feet away.

The gathering quiet
Even muted
Birds in the branches.
We were lost.
We paused,
Unsure of where to turn
In the heavy, white haze.

III.

Then—magically—
The fog crystallized
    before our eyes.
Snow fell—sharp, defined,
Hexagonal tips sticking
    to our hair.
As the snow fell,
The fog lifted,
Raising our spirits with it.
Trees reappeared;
Birds resumed chirping.
Our steps lightened
By renewed sight and sound,
We returned
To the beaten path.

MIDWEST DUO

I.

Fireflies blink in Illinois corn fields,
Like so many tiny Christmas lights.

II.

Minnesota farmhouses,
Surrounded by tree breaks,
Are small islands
Floating in a fertile sea
Of rolling, green fields.

WESTERN HEART

Mountains and oceans
Are my two delights.
Shadowy depths and soaring heights,
Dry air and wet salt water,
Foggy, windswept shores
And dry, high spires—
These contrasts
Are balm to my soul.

I prefer the Pacific Ocean,
Where mountain chains rise
    directly from its shores.
The western half
    of North America
Is my heartland.

Give me
Pacific waves' thunder
And jagged mountains' lightning,
And I am at peace.

WEST YELLOWSTONE, MONTANA

After a thunderstorm
Washes the dust from Montana's air,
You can count the sagebrush
    twenty miles away
And pick out pines on ridges
    forty miles away.

After fierce rain
Has swept across Montana's valleys
And disappeared behind the next mountain ranges,
Everything comes into sharp focus
In the pungent sage-pine air.
Distances are foreshortened;
Mountains jump forward to touch you;
The air shimmers with
    intensely muted colors—
Tan grass, gray sage, dark pine, pale aspen,
Under a brilliant blue sky.

Bulging streams
Rush on with added loads,
Sparkling under the sun's renewed warmth.
High ridges sport
New coats of dusted snow,
As they emerge from turbulent clouds.
Steam rises from highways,
As fleetingly-formed puddles
Evaporate just as quickly.
Glimmering trees
Shake their droplets
In the fresh wind.

You can see one hundred miles of wonder
After a Montana thunderstorm.

BRITISH COLUMBIA

I.

Loon's call
On a still lake
Echoes coyote's howl
From the tree-lined shore.

II.

Lake of glass,
Etched with pine shadows,
Is shattered
By a fish's jump.

III.

Icy mountain stream
Rushes by my windows,
And pulses calmly
In my warm veins.

IV.

Velvet-tan grasses
Carpet dry hills
Sprinkled with
Aspen and pine.

MANNING PROVINCIAL PARK

I.

Shadow-speckled and lupine-lined path,
You wind among the pines
    and summer's splashes
    of day lily, aster, cinquefoil.
Dressed to thrill,
Forest and meadow offset
Your needle-matted
    and root-boned essence.
Pungently perfumed
    by rain-showered pine,
You lay out your summer glory
    in this serene valley
    of cool shadow,
    warm sun,
    and glacial streams.

II.

This peaceful place will not remain.
Its beauty—rock, wood, and water—
    is too intoxicating.
Its quiet is too soothing.
This peaceful place will not remain so;
Yet it is a joy to experience today.

VANCOUVER-VICTORIA DUET

I.

Humpback islands
Swim in the ocean,
Their contours carved
By ancient glaciers.

II.

Slowly, the ferry weaves
A thread of white foam
Through this patchwork of islands.

DRIVING EAST
(TONASKET TO KETTLE FALLS, WA)

Tree-lined highway
    stretches before me.
A quiet continuum of road...
For an hour,
I am alone,
With no one to distract me;
Just the quiet purr of my car
    and the smell of pine.
Chipmunks tempt fate,
    charging across the road.
The air is cool and dry.
The sun-speckled road
Curves downward
    as I top a pass.
Why go back to "civilization?"
This is the land that renews my soul.

ENDINGS...
& NEW
BEGINNINGS

THE OPEN SPIRAL OF LIFE

The Western world
Views life as a line,
Straight and narrow,
Always moving forward
Towards a definite end.

The Eastern world
Views life as a circle,
Birth and death
Uniting to complete
One of many cycles
In one of many lives.

I view life as an open spiral,
Progressing forward,
Yet cycling back
To give new perspectives
To old issues.

Neither static nor narrow,
The spiral contracts or expands
Depending on our responses
To life's internal cycles.

At life's end,
We have two choices—
To spiral inward, slowing,
Until we lose all momentum,
Forming a black hole of the soul,
Or to spiral outward, accelerating,
Until our momentum exceeds
The bounds of this life,
And we break free of this orbit,
Blazing out like a comet
Into another, unimaginable
Galaxy, universe, or life.

SPIRITUAL MIDWIVES

We are midwives of the Spirit.
Gently coaxing,
Strongly massaging,
We talk/sing/cry
Each Soul
Into this life or the next.

We use no drugs.
We have only
    Physical and Spiritual
    Connection
To the birthing soul.

Unlike induced labor,
Natural birth
    of the soul
    Takes Time,
Moves at its own pace—
Sometimes achingly slow,
Sometimes screamingly fast.

We must move
    with the ebb and flow
    of birthing tides.
We cannot rush the labor
    of birth into either life.
We can neither
    hurry birth into this life
    nor prevent birth into the next life.
We simply move with the mother/daughter,
    feeling her pain, joy, grief, anticipation,
    strength, and exhaustion.
And urge her onward
To open to new life,
To free another soul
On its birth-death-day,
To complete life's cycle.

We are midwives of the Spirit
Midway in begendings *
    of a soul's journey.

* *"Begendings"
is a hybrid of
beginnings
and endings.*

— *For Alla*
    Godmother midwife

FOR CORKY

Gentle spirit,
Pass on in Peace.

Your time and calling
Are finished here,
Even though some business
    remains unfinished.

As you move closer
To the Land of Light,
Remember that
    we love you and
    we will miss you deeply, but
    we are letting go of you
    to ease your pain here
    and to ease your journey there.

Sometime surrogate mother
    (when I was three)
And my child's Godmother,
I thank you for
    your tenderness,
    your fierce fight for justice,
    your rock-solid faith,
    your welcoming arms,
    your concern for your children,
    your continuity in my fractured life,
    and your finding humor in all of life.

I am sorry
    that I cannot say "Good-bye and God speed"
    directly to you.
I hope that you will sense
    this brief eulogy of thanks
As your spirit soars
Beyond the majestic mountains
To a New Life and Peace.

                              Amen.

LAST WORDS TO GRANDMOTHER *

Grandmother:

> But why must you
> Become a geologist?
> It is dirty and
> Not-at-all ladylike.

Granddaughter:

> Because you taught your daughters,
> And your daughter taught me,
> To strive for and to excel
> At what I do best.
>
> I may not be ladylike,
> As you would wish,
> But I honor
> Your basic teachings
> By pursuing my calling.

* *To my grandmother, who died of a stroke the day after this phone conversation.*

RETURN HOME *

She returned home
In late summer
For one last time
Before her final slide
Into oblivion.

To sleep with her
Aging black cat
In the four-poster
        cherry bed.

To smell her favorite
Perfume (Woodhue)
Again.

To see the swingset
In the back yard,
Built by her husband
From sturdy steel
        pipes and joints.

To hear the ever-present bluejay
Squawking out the day.

To touch the ivy
Growing on the house brick.

To duck under the dogwood
By the driveway.

For several months now,
She had shuttled
Between home and
The cancer ward.

Gradually, she had said
"goodbye"
To lifelong friends,
To church buddies,

To extended family.
She had tightened her social circle
To immediate family
And an out-of-town priest.
She had let go
Of so much in this life.
("The path to the next life
Is much easier than
The path back to this one.")

Yet she needed
One more return
To her home of twenty years,
To the familiar,
        nonsterile,
        green-with-life
Suburban plot
That she and her family
Had tended until
It flourished with life.

Then she said "goodbye"
And left to face
A new journey
From this life to the next.

The following spring,
She returned in spirit
To see the budding profusion
Of azalea, cherry, crocus, dogwood,
And to tell her family
How much she loved them
Before her full transformation
Into another life.

* Dedicated to my loving and beloved mother, who
wanted her epitaph to be "She did what she could."

FOR MY AUNT

"I must get out of here;
They are coming to get me.
You must help me
Get out of here."

My aunt fidgeted
In her hospice bed.
"Here," she said,
"Massage my legs
So I can get up
And leave."

I kneaded her legs,
Soft and doughy
With retained fluids,
And oddly smelling
Like honeysuckle.

I tried to tell her
That the hospice workers
And her friends
Were her aides,
Not her enemies.

"There's a pharmacy
Around the corner,"
She replied.
"We should be safe there."

Softly, sadly, I explained
That the "enemy"
Was not the people outside,
But the cancer inside.
I wished that I could help,
But the cancer had advanced
        too far.

I had to go,
But, as I left,
I made a point
Of saying,
"I **love** you."

She died
Within four hours.
We raced to give her
A last farewell,
But arrived too late.

Little did I know
The sickly sweet smell
Was the approach
        of Death.

CONTROL

Some infants
Rage at diaper changes,
Sometimes screaming,
Other times fighting
As if in mortal combat.

"It's a control thing.
They hate lack of control."

Some elderly
Rage at nursing care,
Sometimes swearing,
Other times
Throwing tantrums or glasses
As if at war with the world.

"It's a control thing.
They hate lack of control."

THE TOUCH
(QUESTIONS AND ANSWERS)

Q. *Why do you touch his hand?*
You might give him an illness,
Or, worse, vice versa.

A. Because he is a human being.
We all need touch.

Q. *How can you hold his hand?*
It is old, arthritic,
Blotchy, and trembling.

A. Because it is how we connect.
Sight and hearing are failing,
But touch remains.

Q. *How can you stand his touch?*
He is bedridden and unwashed.

A. Because our hands transcend
Outward appearances.
We reach each other's core;
The rest is not important.

Q. *Why do you try to touch?*
He is prone to outbursts and
rages.

A. Because touch is soothing.
Like a child's tantrums,
His rages come from frustration
At lack of self-control.
When we touch, we both soften,
And there is no rage.

Q. *Why do you bother to touch?*
He is an abusive old man.

A. Because, at his core,
Is a decent man,
Who lost his way,
And now lies
Trapped in a body
That is failing him.
Touch, above all else
Recalls that decency.

PRAYER FOR THE DYING

Be reminded
Of your goodness,
Then let go.

SLOW/SUDDEN

Slow death/Sudden death
Which is better?
To linger or not—
      that is the question
Over which we have no control.

To ebb away with a slow tide
Or blaze out in an instant.

To those left behind,
The shock may vary,
But the grief is the same.

UNFINISHED BUSINESS

The hardest part
   of sudden death
   is the shock
   of unfinished business.
No closure.
Just a flaming out
   amidst daily details.
No absolution
   for or from others.
Just the most radical
   paradigm shift.

The hardest part
   of slow death
   is the hard work
   of finishing business.
Of closing emotional accounts.
Of stripping away
   daily details to their essentials.
Of forgiving others
   and oneself
In preparation for the
   Great Transition.

May we end each living day
with minimal unfinished business.

ALL EYES

At birth, we are all eyes,
Everyone—stormy blue-grey,
Soaking in the new-found world
That suddenly exists outside us.

At death, we are all eyes
As the body ebbs away
To free its captive soul
And focus shifts inward
In preparation for entering
   a new world.

GOD SERIES

I.

The Holy Spirit shines
Opalescent fire in my soul.
Her cries for recognition
Burn through my stammering lips.
I blush and fall silent.
How long, O God?
How long
Before we see the other facets of you,
Which were always there?

II.

God is like a benzene ring:
The six sides and double bonds
Present a dynamic, versatile,
        ever-changing image.
The donut-shaped electron clouds
        are the yin-yang glue of Being—
        that can also cloud
        our dim perception.
A balance is required,
        is essential.
While our traditional, patriarchal
        religions have tried
        to see only the yang,
We must recognize the balance of both.

III.

God is a many-faceted gem:
Multi-sided;
With deep color on one side
    and fiery light on another.

IV.

God is Light.
Warm sunshine on a cool day.
Rain-bearing lightning to parched land.
A radiant, brightening Belafonte smile.
Warming fire in a winter night.
Piercing flame that burns
    through inspired souls' eyes.
Night phosphorescence in ocean waves.
Full moonlight on midsummers' eve.
Purple-pink hues of sunset clouds.
Sundogs—the clouds' silver lining.
Irresistible, enveloping lightness-of-being
    who invites us
    to be at One with All.

ANGEL OF DEATH

I am
The Angel of Death.

I ease the way
For souls-in-transition,
Bringing Peace
To fevered brows.

I visit just enough
To guide the dying
In letting go
    of regrets,
    of bitterness,
    of anger,
    of loves,
    of this life,
And relaxing
Into a new Light
    of calm,
    of forgiveness,
    (for and from others),
    of anticipation
    of the next life.

The process of dying
May take hours, days,
    weeks, or months.
Some souls cling to this life
Long enough for my visit.
"I've been waiting for you.
Others have come, but I
Held on for you."

Some souls need time
To loosen bitter knots
Tied to this life,
And to unbind themselves.
"Forgive the others,
Then you can
Forgive yourself."
Words heeded,
The soul can fly freely
To new Hope.

Other souls need time
To untwine loving tendrils
To family or friends
In this life.
"Teach them to release you
By letting go of them."
Words heeded,
The soul can fly freely
To New Life
And to those
Who have gone ahead.

ROSEBUD PHOENIX ALLIANCE

There is a society of souls
Which I call the
"Rosebud Phoenix Alliance,"
Although the name
Is not important.

This alliance is
An earthly network
Of surviving souls
Who have been buried
More than once
By forces beyond our control—
By tragedy, sorrow, grief,
        injustice, or oppression.

And yet,
Through soulful work
Or shear stubbornness,
By wiping away the ashes
Of bitterness or anger or fear
With warm embraces or cleansing tears,
We have risen again,
Renewed, resurrected, reformed,
Bearing roses instead of armor,
Offering love and hope
        instead of rancor,
Bringing bread instead of anger,
Serving wine instead of vinegar,
Recognizing and reconciling
The brokenness of ourselves
        and others,
Healing and revealing
Light to those
Who also live
With Darkness.

Book Order Form

To order additional copies of *The Open Spiral of Life*, please fill out a copy of the form below and mail with a check to:

RIO GATO PRODUCTIONS
P.O. Box 2861-16
Lakewood, CO 80228

TEL/FAX (303) 988-1124

If you wish to use credit cards, please contact a local bookstore or find instructions for internet ordering at:

http://www.sni.net/ ~ hhuyck
(click on <u>poetry</u>)

The Open Spiral of Life BOOK ORDER FORM

Pricing:	1–2 Books .... $14.95 each
	3–5 Books .... $12.00 each
	6 + Books .... Contact Publisher

	Quantity		Unit Cost		Subtotal
Please send me:	_____	x	_____	⟹	_____
Shipping & Handling	"	x	$ 1.75	+	_____
				Subtotal	_____
All Colorado residents pay 3% tax				+	_____
Colorado residents of Lakewood or of the Denver RTD area contact publisher for additional tax rates				+	_____
				TOTAL	_____